ARTEMIS

GODDESS OF THE HUNT AND MOON

Manuela Dunn Mascetti

GODDESS WISDOM

CHRONICLE BOOKS
SAN FRANCISCO

A Labyrinth Book

First published in the United States in 1996 by Chronicle Books.

Copyright © 1996 by Labyrinth Publishing (UK) Ltd.

Design by DW Design.

All rights reserved. No part of this book may be reproduced without written permission from the Publisher.

The Little Wisdom Library–Artemis–Goddess of the Hunt and Moon was produced by Labyrinth Publishing (UK) Ltd. Printed and bound in Hong Kong.

Library of Congress Cataloging-in-Publication Data: Artemis, Goddesses of Wisdom,

Dunn Mascetti, Manuela.

Artemis—Goddess of the Hunt and Moon by Manuela Dunn Mascetti.

p. cm.

Includes bibliographical references.

ISBN 0-8118-0939-0

1. Artemis (Greek deity) I. Title.

BL820. D5D86 1996

292.2' 114—dc20   95-11684
                     CIP

Distributed in Canada by Raincoast Books,
8680 Cambie Street, Vancouver, B.C. V6P 6M9

10 9 8 7 6 5 4 3 2 1

CHRONICLE BOOKS

275 FIFTH STREET, SAN FRANCISCO, CA 94103
CHRONICLE BOOKS ® IS REGISTERED IN THE U.S. PATENT AND TRADEMARK OFFICE.

CONTENTS

INTRODUCTION 9

THE MYTH 15

THE ARCHETYPE 27

THE SYMBOLS 33

THE PATH TO WHOLENESS 39

FRAGMENTATION 43

JOURNEYING THROUGH THE ARCHETYPE: 49

Step 1 – Unity and Multiplicity 50

Step 2 – Transformation and Development 54

Step 3 – Embracing the Goddess 56

BIBLIOGRAPHY 59

FURTHER READING 60

ACKNOWLEDGMENTS 61

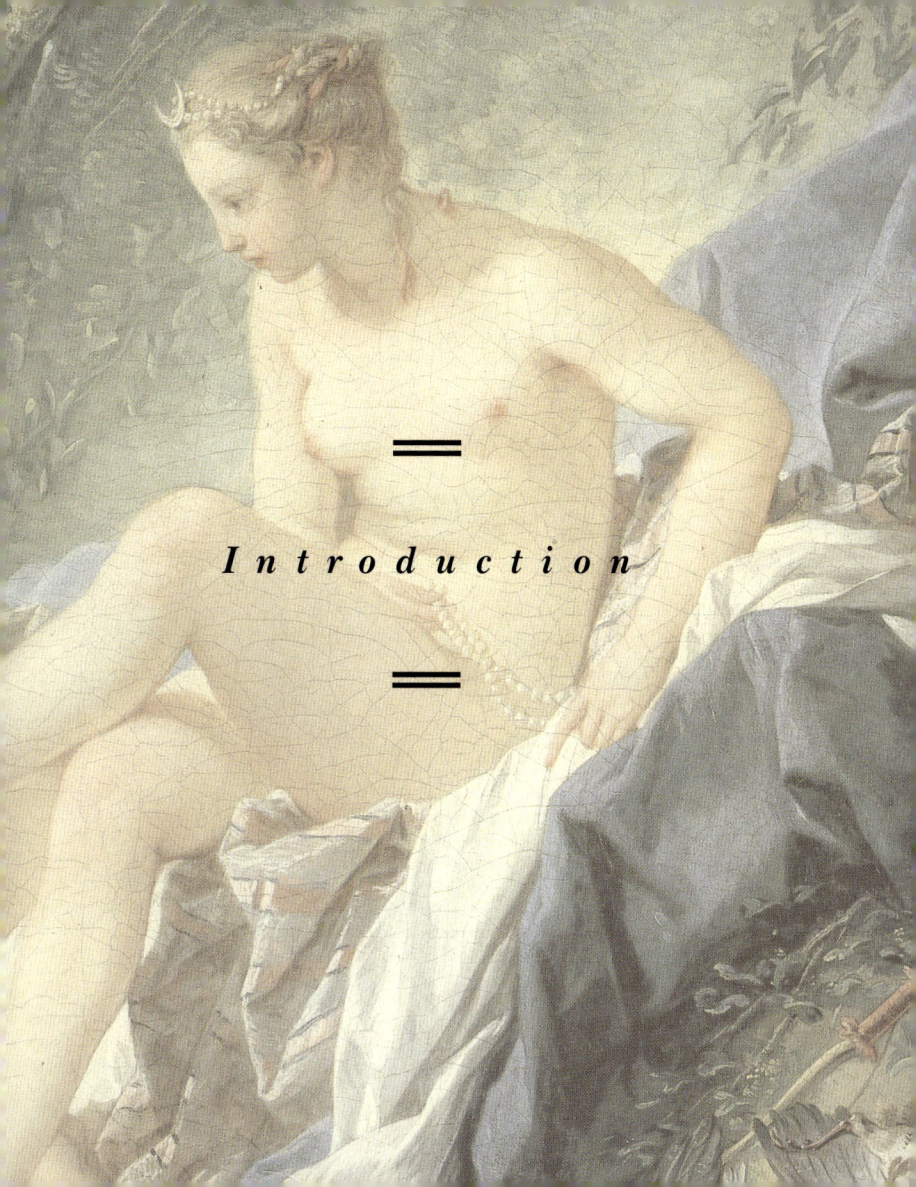

Introduction

ARTEMIS—GODDESS OF THE HUNT AND MOON

When crossing the threshold into the mythology of the goddess, we need to remember that we are entering a psychological and spiritual landscape that is different from everyday life.

The mythological experience is a gateway between the known world, of familiar experiences and responses, and another world entirely, abstract and obtuse. One enters mythological experience without warning or preparation: mythological experience may feel like falling in tune with a powerful, universal rhythm which suddenly moves, guides, and motivates our actions. These moments may be the result of a sacred journey, a dream, a powerful intuition, or healing through therapy. These are all moments when we learn some deep truth about ourselves, when our true natures are revealed and incorporated into a stronger sense of identity. These experiences are so very powerful, so crucial as psychological turning points, that they can never be dismissed. In those deep and sacred moments, woman and goddess merge into one wondrous human divinity.

Artemis was recognized by the ancient Greeks as one of the virgin goddesses, along with Athena and Hestia. These virgin goddesses maintained their independence from male gods—they never married, nor were they raped, seduced, or overpowered by their

INTRODUCTION

Frontispiece: African wooden mask, from the Congo.
Previous pages: A painting by François Boucher (1702–1770) depicting Diana and one of her acolytes at their bath. *Above:* A beautiful Roman fresco of Diana with her bow and arrow on a temple wall in Stabia, near Naples, Italy.

ARTEMIS—GODDESS OF THE HUNT AND MOON

male counterparts on Olympus. Indeed, they bore their divinity alone, carrying out specific functions and roles which were not duplicated by any of the male divinities.

Artemis represents the free and independent feminine spirit, a mode of psychic functioning which is a universal pattern. Carl G. Jung called these trends, which are stored in the collective unconscious, *archetypes*, which, when activated as energy forces in our individual psyches, create a condition by which we are moved very deeply. Artemis, as an archetype, can act as a real force within a woman's psyche. Artemis is ready to blossom forth when we embrace and honor her presence within us.

She rests in that part of ourselves which remains untouched by the need of a partner. When a woman is living out a virgin archetype, she will display characteristics of independence and purity. When exploring the archetype, this psychological virginity (which in the myth appears to be also a physical state) should not be interpreted as a physical or literal virginity; a woman who lives out a virgin archetype will be focused and determined, will travel alone, and set aside time to concentrate on her own needs and desires.

Artemis pulses with life and instinct, and brings a breeze of clean, strong, animal energy. Idealist, mistress of the wilderness, inspired leader, Artemis pursues

INTRODUCTION

her every desire with the spirit of a hunter. Her inquisitive, independent mind and her fresh, direct, bold nature set a new standard for women in the Greek pantheon. Her revolutionary spirit proves that women and goddesses alike can live alone and preside over the wilderness (whether literal or metaphorical). The key word for Artemis is *intuition*: she seeks to understand the underlying thread that links body to mind, instinct to nature, beast to man, and to use this subtle framework as a guide for her own actions and thoughts.

Left: An oil painting by Jules Elie Delaunay (1872) depicting Diana, the Roman name given to Greek Artemis.

The Myth

ARTEMIS—GODDESS OF THE HUNT AND MOON

Artemis was worshipped in ancient Greece as goddess of the hunt, of childbirth, and of the moon. She was the mistress of lonely glades and rivers, and the woodland groves were her sanctuaries. All the beasts that lived in the forests, wild and tame, were sacred to her, and each year, the inhabitants of the forests offered her sacrifices in compensation for all the beasts which they took.

Artemis belongs to the night; darkness, danger, and vibrant, sharpened senses are some of her ancillary qualities. Her virginity guarantees her independence—aloof and untouchable, she is the quintessentially positive goddess. Eternally youthful, dynamic and

sensuous, Artemis represents a powerfully resonant archetype for women today.

The Birth of Artemis

Zeus, chief among the gods and goddesses of Olympus, was unable to restrain himself from making love with the many nymphs descended from the Titans and, after the creation of mankind, with mortal women too. No

THE MYTH

fewer than four great Olympian deities were fathered by him out of wedlock: Hermes, Dionysus, Apollo, and his twin sister Artemis.

Artemis and Apollo were born from the union of Leto and Zeus. When Hera, Zeus's wife, discovered the affair, she was so consumed by jealousy that she sent the serpent Python to pursue pregnant Leto all over the world, and declared that she would not be allowed to give birth in any place where the sun shone. Carried on the wings of the south wind, Leto at last landed on the island of Ortygia, close to Delos, where she gave birth to Artemis. No sooner was the baby girl out of the womb than she helped her mother across the narrow straits to Delos and there, between an olive tree and a date palm growing on the northern side of Mount

Opposite: The head of Artemis adorned coins used during the reign of Pyrrhus (295–272 B.C.) in his capital city Ambracia in the kingdom of Epirus.
Above: Zeus and his daughter Artemis are here sculpted as symbols of power upon the tomb of Cecilia Metella in the Via Appia in Rome.

ARTEMIS—GODDESS OF THE HUNT AND MOON

Cynthus on Delos, Artemis helped Leto give birth to her twin brother Apollo.

Leto had not suffered labor pains when giving birth to Artemis. And because of Artemis's miraculous help with the birth of her brother Apollo, women in ancient Greece used to pray at her temple during pregnancy in order to ensure a painless birth and invoke her powers to help during difficult deliveries.

Right: An oil painting by François Cluet (1510–1572) depicting the goddess at her bath, aided by her virgin acolytes, and entertained by musical satyrs. In the background a knight is riding his horse and keeping away from the sacred ritual. Artemis's hounds are hunting a deer.

THE MYTH

ARTEMIS—GODDESS OF THE HUNT AND MOON

The Childhood of a Goddess

When Artemis was three years old, Leto took her to Mount Olympus to meet her father. Zeus was totally enchanted with his little daughter; he sat her on his lap, and asked what presents she would like.

Pray give me eternal virginity; as many names as my brother Apollo; a bow and arrows like his; the office of bringing light; a saffron hunting tunic with a red hem reaching to my knees; sixty young ocean nymphs, all of the same age, as my maids of honor; twenty river nymphs from Amnisus in Crete, to take care of my buskins and feed my hounds when I am not out shooting; all the mountains in the world; and, lastly, any city you care to choose for me, but one will be enough, because I intend to live on mountains most of the time.

Above (detail) and opposite: The goddess Artemis is here depicted hunting with her magical bow and arrows, helped by her nymphs. Painting by Domenichino, 1617.

20

THE MYTH

ARTEMIS—GODDESS OF THE HUNT AND MOON

Artemis's clear-sighted determination was already apparent as she forged her future, her domains, and areas of responsibility. In Greek mythology it is rare to find an account of a goddess in childhood; most chronicles report the adventures of adult female deities, usually focusing on their affairs with a stronger, seemingly superior male. The only male whom Artemis had to contend with was her father. She made her prerequisites clear: she asked him for gifts, as any little daughter would do, but requested gifts that would set her free and guarantee her total independence. So proud was Zeus of his progeny that he granted little Artemis all her wishes.

THE MYTH

Above: A bison depicted on one of the walls of the Altamira caves (Spain). Artemis was the Greek inheritor of the characteristics of the Paleolithic Lady of the Beasts, worshipped and honored as the main divinity at the time the cave paintings were drawn.

Artemis was eager to try out her newly received gifts. First she traveled widely to find girls to serve as her attendants; then she visited the Cyclopes on the island of Lipara, who were hammering away in their smithies making tools for the gods. Artemis asked them to make her a silver bow and arrows, in return for which she offered them the first animal she killed. Next, she went to Arcadia, where Pan gave her three lop-eared hounds strong enough to drag live lions back to their kennels, and seven of the fastest running dogs from Sparta. Thus equipped, Artemis was set to become the most famed hunter on Olympus. Soon she captured two horned stags, which she harnessed to a golden chariot and drove north to

ARTEMIS—GODDESS OF THE HUNT AND MOON

Mount Olympus, where she cut her first torch and lit it from the ashes of a tree which had been struck by lighting, and eventually she returned home, where her nymphs unyoked the stags and fed them on trefoil.

The Deeds of Artemis

Artemis lived in the woods and glades of Olympus, guarding Nature by day and hunting at night with her pack of hounds. The goddess's rule over her domain was reflective of the virginal qualities of the archetype: she was independent and strong-willed. She expected the same degree of perfect chastity from her companions that she practiced herself.

Artemis was always associated with her twin brother Apollo, the god of light. She was worshipped as the goddess of moonlight, and she presided over women's mysteries, such as birth, death, and renewal. Both she and Apollo acted as patrons to musicians, and they presided over the choir and dances at Delphi.

Although Artemis was chaste, she once fell in love with the hunter Orion. She might even have married him had her brother Apollo not intervened. One day when Orion was bathing in the sea, he swam so far from the shore that he became almost invisible. Having watched Orion swim out, Apollo challenged Artemis to shoot at the distant object which

THE MYTH

moved on the surface of the waves. Artemis, not realizing that she would be aiming at her beloved Orion, accepted Apollo's challenge and shot. Her arrow pierced Orion's temple, and he drowned.

Above: Artemis and her twin brother Apollo come to the rescue of warriors and are here immortalized in a frieze in Delphi, Greece (c. 525 B.C.).

ARTEMIS—GODDESS OF THE HUNT AND MOON

In practical terms, the virgin qualities of the archetype enable a woman to feel whole without a man supporting her. She will be happy to pursue her own interests without needing the approval of others, striving to be recognized as an equal in a male-dominated environment.

When three-year-old Artemis asked Zeus for gifts which would guarantee her independence, she demonstrated a remarkably clear vision of the course of her own life. So it is with women in whom the Artemis archetype is active. Their ability to achieve their goals and to make their dreams come true goes beyond mere good fortune. One of the greatest gifts the archetype brings is the ability to focus on an inner desire and make it come true.

Artemis's ability to sight prey represents the gift to discriminate between what is wanted and what is really needed. She concentrates on her prey, knowing how to wait and when to strike. In the same way, Artemis energy will compel one to wait for the exact moment before taking any action, thus preserving power. This attitude means that a woman will seldom fail to get what she wants and needs.

Opposite: A fourth-century B.C. jar in the form of a fawn, one of the constant symbols associated with Artemis.

THE ARCHETYPE

ARTEMIS—GODDESS OF THE HUNT AND MOON

The Qualities of Artemis

☽ Virginal, independent: this woman feels complete without a partner in her life or a family surrounding her

☽ Goal-oriented, focused: able to pursue her dreams and make them come true

☽ Intuitive, with good judgment: is often impulsive, but when she trusts her instincts, is rarely wrong

☽ Inspirational: an excellent and trustworthy leader, eager to help others in pursuing their ideals

☽ Blunt and fierce: can overreact and turn vengeful when her independence or integrity is threatened, or when traditionally feminine roles are imposed upon her

☽ Solitary and self-sufficient: needs space, easily feels trapped and claustrophobic, both physically and psychologically

☽ Adventurous and ambitious: has a deep desire for travel and exploration, both physical and spiritual

THE ARCHETYPE

Above: A statue of many-breasted Artemis found at Ephesus, one of the goddess's main centers of worship. Although in Greek mythology she was venerated as a virgin goddess, Artemis was also worshipped in her second person, as orgiastic Nymph, recallingthe Cretal, "Lady of the Wild Things" and the ancient goddesses of Mesopotamia, Ishtar and Astarte, from whom she was descended.

The Symbols

ARTEMIS—GODDESS OF THE HUNT AND MOON

The gifts Artemis asks her father for are symbols which, when unraveled, become the fundamental milestones of the life of a virgin woman. The gift of eternal virginity, for instance, stands for the wish to always remain "true to her nature." When this archetype is active in a woman, she cannot enter a relationship, whether with a lover, a friend, or a working partner, in which she would have to compromise her true self. Her uncontaminated nature is often the mirror for the faults and corruption of others, even though this reflection may be totally unintended. In fact, the name Artemis means "water," which reflects reality back to the onlooker.

Artemis asks Zeus for bows and

arrows. The shooting of the arrows is symbolic of the expression of the self: the arrows represent wishes, actions, decisions. The bow is a metaphor for the new moon, symbol of the maiden: an expres-

THE SYMBOLS

Previous pages: The Queen of the Night, a set design for the Berlin production of Mozart's *The Magic Flute,* drew inspiration from the symbols of Artemis. *Opposite and above:* The moon is a recurring attribute of Artemis, symbolizing intuition and the power of the night forces.

sion of intuition and mystery. Her wishes and decisions, therefore, can be seen to spring from an instinctive rather than a logical source. The archetype may engender a lack of ability of logically explaining the reasons behind her actions, but she intuits that they are right.

The moon is thus a potent and revealing symbol of Artemis. The goddess had the right to feed her animals on trefoil, a symbol of the ancient lunar trinity. And in ancient rituals, the priestesses devoted to Artemis wore masks of luminous white clay, recalling the presence of the moon (and so Artemis) in their lives.

ARTEMIS—GODDESS OF THE HUNT AND MOON

The Symbols of the Goddess

The Stag

In Paleolithic caves there are representations of shamans garbed as stags—because of the annual renewal of its antlers, the stag was compared in many cultures to the tree of life. The stag was also a symbol of fertility, revered as a conductor of souls to the other world, as representative of death and renewal.

The Bee

Bees primarily symbolize diligence and social organization. Artemis's priestesses were sometimes called bees, with reference to the virginity of the worker bees.

Bow and Arrow

They are symbols of war and power, and also of instinct, intuition, and hope. The bow often refers to vigor and vitality, feminine energy; the arrow is a symbol of swiftness, ambition, and intellect.

Above: Bees were often depicted flying around Artemis, symbols of her virginal acolytes.
Opposite page: Artemis the Hunter is here immortalized in a floor mosaic found in a Roman villa in Tunisia (second century A.D.).

THE SYMBOLS

The Path to Wholeness

ARTEMIS—GODDESS OF THE HUNT AND MOON

The myths of the goddesses provide some wonderfully inspiring material, providing strong, complete images of archetypal woman. Goddesses embodied those qualities that we all strive to emulate and incarnate within ourselves, and through developing a full understanding of the myth, we find patterns which echo our own spiritual growth. Some women may recognize aspects of Artemis within themselves—determination, perhaps, or independence—but may be less familiar with other parts of the archetype—the wild, instinctual, lunar nature of the goddess. In order to embrace the archetype fully, we must recognize those areas in our psyche that are empty or fragmented.

The retelling of Greek myths awakens within us awareness of the existence of personal myth—the power to create and define one's own story as one progresses through life. If we see ourselves as spiritual beings journeying through life, then the metaphors and symbols in the stories of the goddesses seem all the more tangible. Personal myths resonate with collective myths of an older time; the archetype of Artemis is activated in our psyche when we feel independent, ardent,

THE PATH TO WHOLENESS

strong. Myths are ultimately pieces of our fragmented self. They represent aspects and characteristics of our personality, some of which may be eclipsed from consciousness, some of which may be damaged and distorted. These fragments must all be healed and reunited if we are to become whole. It is by understanding and integrating the archetypes inherited from ancient times that we regain our wholeness, bridging modern needs with ancient wisdom. A new self thus emerges, a spiritual center of a woman's personality that gives meaning and nourishment to both inner and outer life.

Opposite: The goddess Artemis, a frieze adorning the walls of the Parthenon on the Acropolis (Phidias, 447–422 B.C.). *Above:* A Renaissance tarot card depicting a virgin holding the crescent moon—two symbols belonging to Artemis that were inherited by a later age.

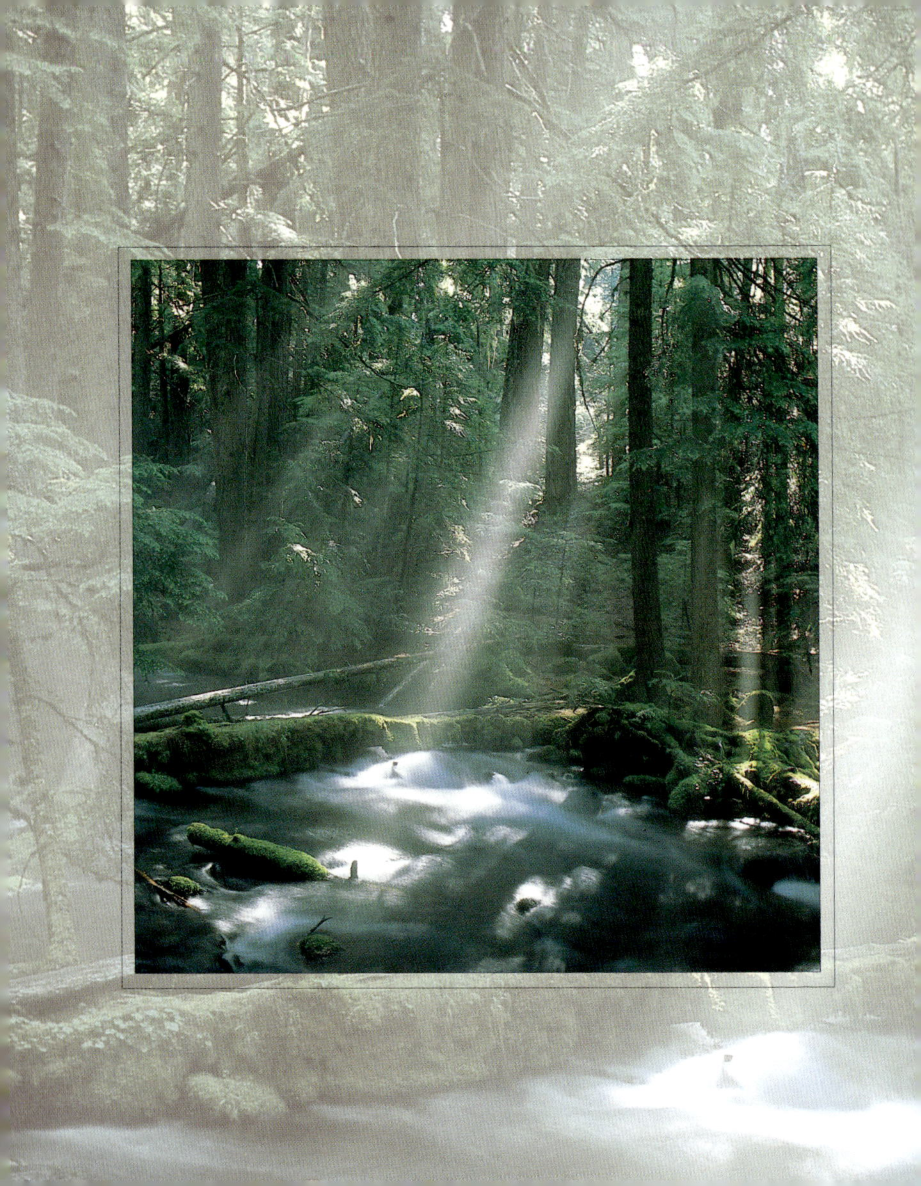

Fragmentation

ARTEMIS—GODDESS OF THE HUNT AND MOON

The danger with all virginal archetypes is that, when acted out, they can be affected by less than pure courses: rejection of life, the pursuit of stereotypical masculine goals, or a streak of masochism and dissatisfaction.

The psychological difficulties of women who identify with Artemis may stem from their extreme focus on achievement. Artemis seems to catch any prey she sets her sight on, which could lead us to believe that one should always be in control, an attitude often accompanied by contempt for weakness or vulnerability. Problems arise when one is compelled to win for the sake of winning, rather than for the enjoyment of the goal or of the race. The Artemis energy needs to be challenged and constantly stimulated by new goals, or utter boredom may drown the woman in whom this archetype is active.

Above: An allegorical wild animal—Artemis was worshipped as the Goddess of Wilderness who did not tame animals and yet was their mistress.
Opposite: A modern carnival mask, an inheritance of ancient rituals in honor of Artemis, during which her priestesses wore clay masks to symbolize the moon.

FRAGMENTATION

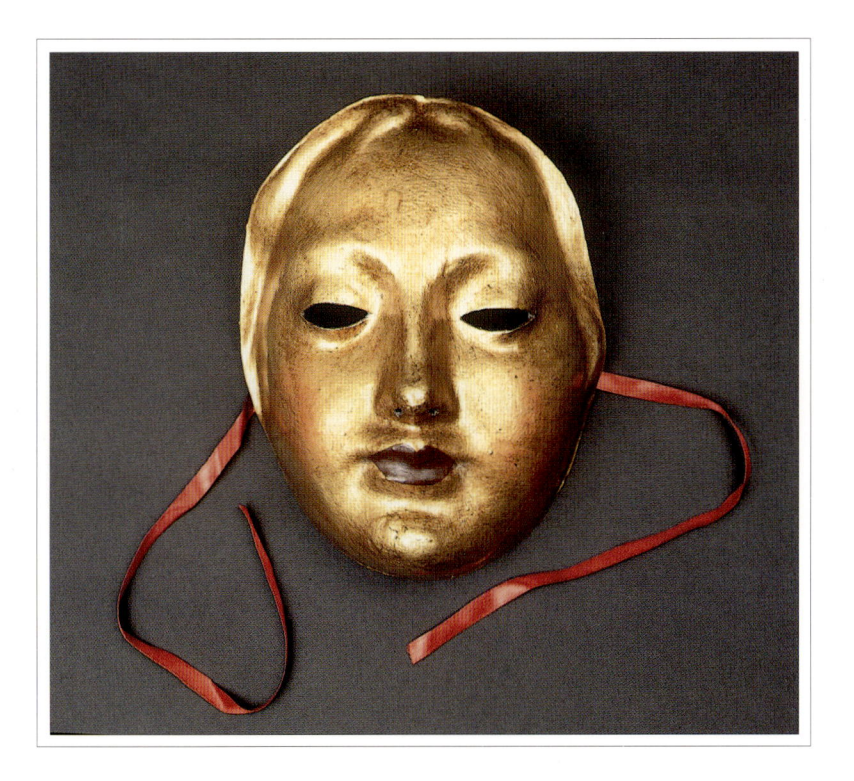

ARTEMIS—GODDESS OF THE HUNT AND MOON

Artemis lived freely in the forests, doing whatever pleased her. She was never victimized, and she took instant, effective revenge on all who dared disturb her. We read here a lack of compassion and a streak of pure selfishness: there exists a frozen spot within her which refuses to accept fault, weakness, or doubt. She judges others harshly in order to protect the wounded self, and like a judge, this point in her personality imparts sentences and punishments, and is highly critical. When this energy grips our psyche we may feel disillusioned with life—nothing is quite good enough. There seems little point in making an effort if we are only going to be disappointed again and again. We cease to try, and nothing happens and we continue the vicious circle. In the myth, Artemis fled Olympus and lived in the seclusion of wilderness, only accepting the company of women who were subordinate to her. We need to be careful not to seclude ourselves within our own wilderness out of our mistaken disillusionment with society. If we do our work, creativity and fulfillment will reenter our lives, warmth and humanity will color our relationships, and the deep mysteries of our self will start flowering within our hearts again.

Opposite: A faun playing the flute—Artemis and her twin brother Apollo were worshipped as patrons of musicians.

FRAGMENTATION

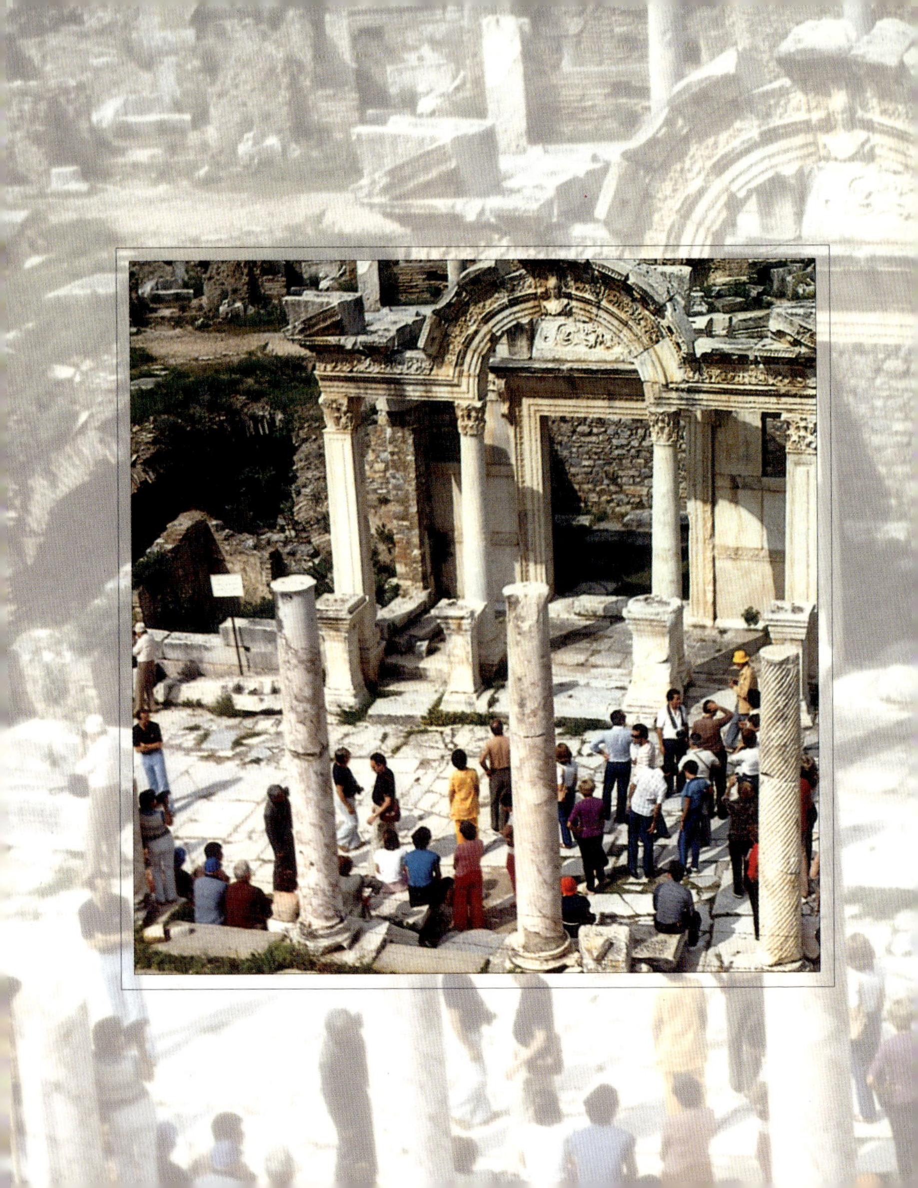

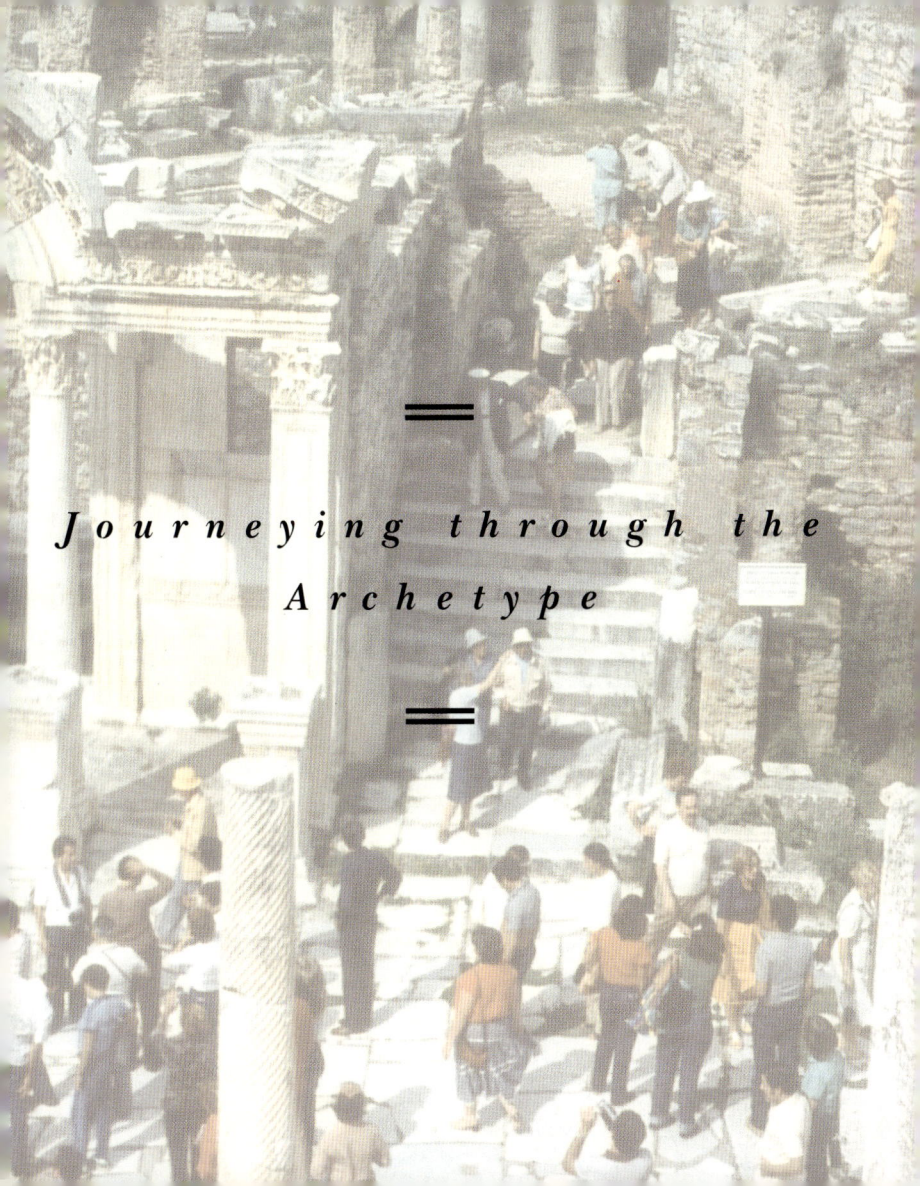

Journeying through the Archetype

ARTEMIS—GODDESS OF THE HUNT AND MOON

Step 1

Unity and Multiplicity

Myths and legends present us with a complete picture. Artemis carried the vestiges of an earlier fertility goddess, worshipped since prehistory as the Lady of the Beasts. With time, she became a virgin goddess, proud, independent, and strong. She used a silver bow to hunt for her prey; she presided over wildlife and came to the aid of women in childbirth. As an archetype, Artemis is the sister of the women's movement; clear

Right: An elk bellowing mating calls in the morning mist—elk, fawns, and deer were sacred animals of Artemis.

JOURNEYING THROUGH THE ARCHETYPE

and discriminating, determinedly promoting the social change that will rescue her companions from the unfair burden of patriarchy.

Unity for the woman in whom this archetype is active entails integrating the body and the mind. If we give value to the mind and repress the body, we will start creating shadows within us which will, sooner or later, take revenge at a psychic level. In the intellectualizing of feelings and relationships, the body remains cruelly left behind. Unity emerges when the body and the mind become close, resonating to the same rhythm.

When this unity is successfully achieved, multiplicity emerges. Artemis is a wonderfully rich

Above: La Danse by Matisse. In ancient Greece, sacred dancing rituals and sacrifices were performed every year in honor of Artemis, in compensation for all the beasts that were killed in her forests.

JOURNEYING THROUGH THE ARCHETYPE

archetype. Lover of nature, independent, warm-hearted and yet discriminating, Artemis turns a woman into the most supportive friend, an inspiration. Concentration on the body, nourishment of the physical spirit through dance, perhaps, or close contact with nature, relaxes the mind and brings about a natural healing to the split between body and soul. This dialogue needs to be maintained constantly in order not to atrophy the instincts the Artemis energy bestows upon us. In order to be able to express and be nourished by multiplicity, we need to care for the gifts of our spirit—our intuition, determination, and natural generosity can be stifled all too easily under the weight of careless living.

Step 2

Transformation and Development

Transformation, achieving the fullness of the self, is a slow, gradual process. The unconscious keeps its door very tightly closed. We need grace and positivity in order to shine light upon that particular room of our psyche. We may want to revisit our childhood ambitions and dreams, to find that little girl again who was so happy then. We might need to ask her what happened in the process of growing up, and ask whether we can help. As we explore different parts of our forgotten self, so we will notice the Artemis confidence growing within us, giving us strength.

Development is a continuum which becomes progressively more significant as we become able to articulate our process. Keeping a journal, facing a mirror of the psyche each day, is one of the best ways to awaken our sense of wonder at the process of life. We discover that Artemis is there, hunting for new possibilities. If we pay close attention, dreams become realities, realities become dreamlike. The soul begins to communicate and guide, and our responsibility towards her grows stronger.

Opposite: A stone relief depicting Artemis and her bear priestesses; Dura-Europos, Syria, second century B.C.

JOURNEYING THROUGH THE ARCHETYPE

ARTEMIS—GODDESS OF THE HUNT AND MOON

Step 3

Embracing the Goddess

The goddess is a fluid presence who does not abdicate her throne by becoming the plaything of other gods: Artemis bears her divinity with strength and grace. If we are able to recognize her presence, we must start behaving like a goddess, intimately in touch with our being, discriminating between what we think we want and what we really want. Artemis as a child of three set her own standards. Let us also be true to our souls and not accept that which does not respect our essential quality. The psychic adoption of virginity is the ability to discern and respect our essential nature so that we are able to defend it when it is endangered.

Above: A stone relief depicting Artemis and her sacred hunting hounds, c. 400 B.C.

JOURNEYING THROUGH THE ARCHETYPE

The interplay of body and mind is the true source of nourishment for the Artemis woman. In this dialogue, consciousness becomes progressively more transparent, and so our wisdom increases, strengthening and revitalizing us along the way. If we avoid rigidity and work to unveil our own individuality, Artemis will honor us and bring to us the bounty of the goddess.

Right: The goddess Artemis.

ARTEMIS—GODDESS OF THE HUNT AND MOON

BIBLIOGRAPHY

Graves, R. *The Greek Myths.* London: Penguin Books, 1992.

Harding, E. M. *Woman's Mysteries.* New York and San Francisco: Harper & Row, 1971.

Jung, C. G. *Man and His Symbols.* London: Aldous Books, 1964.

Neumann, E. *The Great Mother.* New York: Bollingen Foundation, Princeton University Press, 1963.

Walker, B. *The Woman's Encyclopedia of Myths and Secrets.* San Francisco: HarperSanFrancisco, 1991.

FURTHER READING

Bolen, J. Shinoda. *Goddesses in Everywoman.* New York and San Francisco: Harper & Row Publishers, 1984.

Bolen, J. Shinoda. *Crossing to Avalon.* San Francisco: HarperSanFrancisco, 1994.

Estés, C. Pinkola. *Women Who Run with the Wolves.* New York: Ballantine Books, 1992.

Harding, E. M. *Woman's Mysteries.* New York and San Francisco: Harper & Row, 1971.

Perera, S. Brinton. *Descent to the Goddess—A Way of Initiation for Women.* Toronto: Inner City Books, 1981.

Woodman, M. *The Pregnant Virgin—A Process of Psychological Transformation.* Toronto: Inner City Books, 1985.

Woodman, M. *Leaving My Father's House—A Journey to Conscious Femininity.* London: Ebury Press, 1993

ACKNOWLEDGMENTS

Picture Acknowledgments

AKG London, pages: 8; 13; 19; 21; 32; 34; 40; 45; 57ó *Diana of Gabii, Louvre.*

The Complete Picture, pages: 35; 42; 51.

C M Dixon Photo Resources, pages: 16; 17; 25; 37.

E T Archive, pages: 11; 29; 41; 47—sculpture by Marcello Mascherini; 55; 56; 58—watch case, 18th century.

Range Pictures Ltd., pages: 4; 22; 44—*Allegory,* by Ben Shahn; 52.

Tony Stone Images, pages: 7; 14; 26; 36; 38.

Turkish Embassy, pages: 31; 48—Temple of Artemis, Ephesus.

Text Acknowledgments

The quotes that appear in this book are taken from *The Greek Myths* by Robert Graves (published by Penguin Books, 1992), reprinted here by kind permission of Carcanet Press Limited.